EXPLORING THE STATES

California

THE GOLDEN STATE

by Emily Schnobrich

BELLWETHER MEDIA · MINNEAPOLIS, MN

Note to Librarians, Teachers, and Parents:

Blastoff! Readers are carefully developed by literacy experts and combine standards-based content with developmentally appropriate text.

Level 1 provides the most support through repetition of high-frequency words, light text, predictable sentence patterns, and strong visual support.

Level 2 offers early readers a bit more challenge through varied simple sentences, increased text load, and less repetition of high-frequency words.

Level 3 advances early-fluent readers toward fluency through increased text and concept load, less reliance on visuals, longer sentences, and more literary language.

Level 4 builds reading stamina by providing more text per page, increased use of punctuation, greater variation in sentence patterns, and increasingly challenging vocabulary.

Level 5 encourages children to move from "learning to read" to "reading to learn" by providing even more text, varied writing styles, and less familiar topics.

Whichever book is right for your reader, Blastoff! Readers are the perfect books to build confidence and encourage a love of reading that will last a lifetime!

This edition first published in 2014 by Bellwether Media, Inc.

No part of this publication may be reproduced in whole or in part without written permission of the publisher.
For information regarding permission, write to Bellwether Media, Inc., Attention: Permissions Department,
5357 Penn Avenue South, Minneapolis, MN 55419.

Library of Congress Cataloging-in-Publication Data

Schnobrich, Emily.
  California / by Emily Schnobrich.
    pages cm – (Blastoff! readers. Exploring the states)
  Includes bibliographical references and index.
  Summary: "Developed by literacy experts for students in grades three through seven, this book introduces young readers
to the geography and culture of California"–Provided by publisher.
  ISBN 978-1-62617-0049 (hardcover : alk. paper)
  1. California–Juvenile literature. I. Title.
  F861.3.S37 2014
  979.4–dc23

                                                      2013002382

Printed in the United States of America, North Mankato, MN.

Table of Contents

Where Is California?

California sits on the West Coast of the United States. Covering 158,608 square miles (410,793 square kilometers), it is the third largest state. Only Texas and Alaska are larger. California has a long, slender shape. It stretches from the northern United States all the way to the country of Mexico in the south.

California is neighbors with Oregon to the north. Its eastern border touches Nevada and Arizona. To the west lies the great Pacific Ocean. The capital city, Sacramento, is located in northern California.

Pacific Ocean

N

W

E

S

Oregon

Nevada

Sacramento

San Francisco

San Jose

California

Death Valley

Los Angeles

Arizona

San Diego

Mexico

History

For thousands of years, **Native** Americans lived off the land that is now California. Spanish explorers were the first Europeans to settle the area. In 1822, Mexico took control of the land. James Marshall discovered gold near Sacramento in 1848. Thousands of people rushed there with the hope of becoming rich. Two years later, California became a state. Many **immigrants** later traveled there to build the **transcontinental** railroad. California is now one of the most **diverse** parts of the country.

Did you know?
People who traveled to California in 1849 to search for gold were called "forty-niners."

California Timeline!

1769: Spanish settlers arrive in San Diego.

1822: Mexico takes control of California.

1846-1848: Mexico and the United States go to war over land. The United States wins land that includes California.

1848: Gold is discovered in northern California.

1850: California becomes the thirty-first state.

1869: The construction of the first transcontinental railroad is finished.

1906: A major earthquake destroys much of San Francisco.

1930s: Dry, windy weather destroys farms on the Great Plains. Many families move west to California.

1937: The Golden Gate Bridge opens.

Mexican-American War

transcontinental railroad

1906 earthquake

The Land

California is covered in mountains and hills. In the northwest, the Klamath Mountains stretch down from Oregon. To the northeast is the **volcanic** Cascade Range. The Coast Ranges run along California's western coast. The Sierra Nevada lines its eastern border. Between these two ranges lies the flat Central Valley.

The Salton Sea is the largest of California's many lakes. The Sacramento and other rivers cross the land. Southern California is home to the Mojave and Colorado Deserts. Several islands lie off the coast. Hot and dry weather is common in the south. The rest of the state is mild and cool.

fun fact

Around 10,000 earthquakes shake southern California every year! However, most of them are too small to notice.

Yosemite National Park

California's Climate
average °F

spring
Low: 47°
High: 69°

summer
Low: 58°
High: 83°

fall
Low: 50°
High: 73°

winter
Low: 40°
High: 59°

Did you know?
Yosemite National Park was the first area of land set aside by the U.S. government for preservation and protection.

Death Valley

Did you know?

In the summer, temperatures in Death Valley can reach over 120 degrees Fahrenheit (49 degrees Celsius)!

Death Valley is a long, deep valley surrounded by mountains. It lies in southeastern California near the Nevada border. It is the lowest point in the United States. The valley is a strange place with very hot, dry weather. Spectacular sand **dunes** and **craters** cover the north end of the valley. The sparkling Saratoga **Springs** are in the south.

Very little rain falls in the valley. Still, thousands of colorful wildflowers blanket the land in springtime. In the late 1800s, Californians came to the valley to dig up gold, borax, and other valuable **minerals**. Visitors to Death Valley National Park can explore the **ghost towns** they left behind.

Saratoga Springs

! fun fact

The Saratoga Springs give life to animals found nowhere else in the world. One example is the silvery blue Saratoga Springs pupfish.

Wildlife

California is home to fascinating wildlife. Coyotes, rattlesnakes, and tortoises are just a few of the animals that roam the deserts. Deer, mountain lions, and black bears live in the forests and hills. The ocean is filled with tuna, squid, and **migrating** whales. Pelicans, hawks, and bluebirds fly overhead.

Cactuses and yucca plants thrive in the deserts. Wildflowers such as fiddlenecks and California poppies are common in the hills. California's most famous plant is the great redwood tree. Redwoods are the tallest trees in the world. Some grow more than 300 feet (90 meters) tall and can be 10 to 20 feet (3 to 6 meters) wide.

tortoise

rattlesnake

mountain lion

Did you know?
California's state animal, the California grizzly bear, is extinct.

! fun fact

Some redwood trees are more than 1,500 years old!

Landmarks

Golden Gate Bridge

Natural beauty is one of the most charming parts of California. Redwood trees line the coast of northern California like giant soldiers. Many are protected in Redwood National Park. On Venice Beach, flashy street performers play music and do magic tricks for people walking by.

Lake Tahoe is a popular vacation spot. This large, shimmering mountain lake lies on the Nevada border. One of California's most familiar landmarks is the Golden Gate Bridge. This deep orange bridge crosses the Golden Gate **Strait** between San Francisco and Marin County. It was designed to survive earthquakes and strong winds that sweep over the Pacific Ocean.

fun fact

Disneyland in Anaheim is a famous theme park. It is full of exciting rides and "lands" where strange adventures and Disney characters come to life.

Los Angeles

Los Angeles lies on the coast in southern California. It is the second largest city in the United States after New York City. Unlike other huge cities, L.A. doesn't have many tall skyscrapers. Heavy traffic, **smog**, and earthquakes are some of L.A.'s most challenging features. However, the city is also home to beautiful sandy beaches and snowy mountains.

L.A. is known for its web of **suburbs**. Hollywood is the most famous of these. It is the center of the American movie-making business. **Tourists** try to spot their favorite celebrities strolling the streets of Los Angeles.

Hollywood

Did you know?

More than three million people of all backgrounds live in L.A. The city is home to the largest population of Mexicans outside of Mexico.

California is the United States' top farming state. Farmers grow nuts, cotton, and decorative trees and plants. They also raise cows and chickens. Many Californians make electronics and computer equipment. Some drill into the ground for natural gas and oil.

Off the coast, fishers catch tuna, squid, and other sea creatures. Most Californians have **service jobs**. Some are lawyers and doctors. Those who work in hotels and restaurants serve the millions of tourists who visit the state each year. Many moviemakers are based in the state, too.

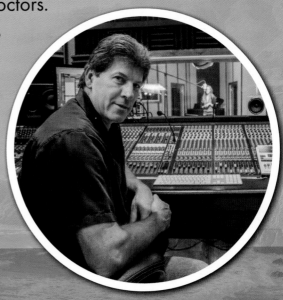

Where People Work in California

manufacturing
7%

farming and
natural resources
2%

government
13%

services
78%

Playing

fun fact

Los Angeles hosted the Summer Olympics in 1932 and again in 1984.

Californians enjoy spending time in the sun. They surf, sail, and swim in the ocean. The state's mountains are good for hiking. Some are snowy enough to ski on. Golf and tennis are other popular outdoor activities. Californians also love professional sports. Los Angeles alone has six major sports teams.

Walt Disney Concert Hall

Museums are a great way to escape the heat. The California State Railroad Museum is a popular stop in Sacramento. Californians also go to theaters to enjoy concerts and plays. The Los Angeles Philharmonic orchestra performs at the Walt Disney Concert Hall.

Peach Salsa

Ingredients:

6 fresh peaches, chopped

2 green onions, sliced thin, including tops

2 tablespoons lime juice

2 teaspoons chopped fresh cilantro

2 teaspoons garlic chili sauce

1/2 teaspoon five spice powder

1/4 teaspoon white pepper

Directions:

1. Mix all ingredients in a bowl.

2. Chill before serving.

3. Serve as a salsa with tortilla chips or on top of meat.

sushi

Did you know?
Californians love to eat raw fish! Sushi is a Japanese cuisine. It features rice with raw seafood, seaweed, and other ingredients.

Napa Valley

! fun fact
Vineyards in Napa Valley and Sonoma Valley grow grapes to make world-famous wines.

Many unique foods grow well in California's warm weather. Lemons, oranges, and avocados hang from trees. Crisp lettuce, tomatoes, and most other vegetables sprout from the ground. People can buy these fresh ingredients from farmers' markets all year long.

Californians enjoy a variety of **cuisines**, including Mexican and Korean food. Fresh seafood from the Pacific Ocean is also popular. Californians love to stop at food trucks that line the streets. These four-wheeled kitchens sell tacos, sandwiches, and other quick snacks for meals on the go.

23

custom car show

Nice cars are a big deal in California. During the summer, fans go to weekend shows to admire classic and **custom** cars. Californians also hold events to celebrate music, seafood, wine, and movies. The American Film Institute Fest in Hollywood shows new movies from all over the world.

The Tournament of Roses takes place on the first day of
January in Pasadena. It is a gigantic celebration of sports
and beauty to welcome the New Year. The day starts
with a parade of floats decorated in blooming flowers.
Later, two of the best college football teams in the nation
compete for a trophy in the Rose Bowl.

Hollywood

Hollywood is the heart of American show business. Many movie and music stars live in the surrounding neighborhoods. Even the sidewalks of Hollywood Boulevard are famous. They are covered in stone stars that hold the names of famous entertainers.

Visitors to Hollywood can check out Universal Studios. They enjoy movie-themed rides and learn how films are made. Hollywood is also known for its many performance **venues**. The Hollywood Bowl is used for outdoor concerts. The beautiful Chinese Theater on Hollywood Boulevard often hosts movie **premieres**. Hollywood is a symbol of the creative ideas and colorful people that make up the Golden State.

fun fact !

The huge white Hollywood sign that sits on Mount Lee first said "Hollywoodland." Each letter is 45 feet (14 meters) tall!

Chinese Theater

Fast Facts About California

California's Flag

The California flag is white with a thick red stripe across the bottom. Above the stripe is a California grizzly bear and the words "California Republic." A red star dots the upper left corner.

State Flower
California poppy

State Nickname:	The Golden State
State Motto:	"Eureka" (I Have Found It)
Year of Statehood:	1850
Capital City:	Sacramento
Other Major Cities:	Los Angeles, San Diego, San Francisco, San Jose
Population:	37,253,956 (2010)
Area:	158,608 square miles (410,793 square kilometers); California is the 3rd largest state.
Major Industries:	farming, fishing, electronics, food processing, tourism
Natural Resources:	oil, natural gas, boron
State Government:	80 representatives; 40 senators
Federal Government:	53 representatives; 2 senators
Electoral Votes:	55

State Animal
California grizzly bear

State Bird
California quail

Extinct in California
since 1922

Glossary

craters—bowl-shaped dips in the land

cuisines—styles of cooking unique to certain areas or groups of people

custom—made special or different from others

diverse—made up of many people from many different backgrounds

dunes—hills of sand

ghost towns—abandoned towns or villages

immigrants—people who leave one country to live in another country

migrating—traveling from one place to another, often with the seasons

minerals—natural substances found in the earth

native—originally from a specific place

premieres—the first showings of movies, plays, or other performances

service jobs—jobs that perform tasks for people or businesses

smog—fog made up of pollution

springs—areas where water flows up through cracks in the earth

strait—a narrow stretch of water that connects two larger bodies of water

suburbs—communities that lie just outside a city

tourists—people who travel to visit another place

transcontinental—crossing the continent

venues—places that hold events such as concerts

volcanic—relating to volcanoes; a volcano is a hole in the earth that spews hot, melted rock.

To Learn More

AT THE LIBRARY
Duffield, Katy S. *California History for Kids: Missions, Miners, and Moviemakers in the Golden State*. Chicago, Ill.: Chicago Review Press, 2012.

Kennedy, Teresa. *California*. New York, N.Y.: Children's Press, 2008.

Raum, Elizabeth. *The California Gold Rush: An Interactive History Adventure*. Mankato, Minn.: Capstone Press, 2008.

ON THE WEB
Learning more about California is as easy as 1, 2, 3.

1. Go to www.factsurfer.com.

2. Enter "California" into the search box.

3. Click the "Surf" button and you will see a list of related Web sites.

With factsurfer.com, finding more information is just a click away.

Index